Teach Me About
Potty Training

Written by Joy Berry
Illustrated by Dana Regan

Every person goes peepee.

Every person goes poopoo.

I go peepee and poopoo too.

Sometimes I go peepee and poopoo in my pants.

My pants get wet and dirty.

When my pants get wet and dirty, it smells bad.

I feel uncomfortable wearing wet and dirty pants.

I do not like to go peepee and poopoo in my pants.

Other people do not like it when I go peepee and poopoo in my pants.

There is a special thing in which I can go peepee and poopoo.

It is called a toilet.

I am careful around the toilet.

The toilet is in the bathroom.

Bathrooms away from home are often called restrooms.

There is a restroom almost everywhere I go.

There are restrooms in stores, restaurants, gas stations, and parks.

There are restrooms in schools, libraries, and theaters.

There is always a toilet for me to use in every restroom.

MEN

The toilet makes a loud noise when I flush it.

The noise scares me.

I tell someone that the noise scares me.

That person lets me flush the toilet over and over again.

I get used to the sound.

It does not scare me anymore.

I am scared that I might fall into the toilet.

I tell someone that I am scared.

That person shows me how to sit on the toilet.

I lean forward and hold on with both hands so that I will feel safe.

I put toilet paper into the toilet bowl.

I flush it.

The toilet paper goes away and does not come back.

That scares me.

It makes me wonder if the toilet might take me away, too.

I tell someone that I am scared that the toilet might take me away.

That person shows me the hole inside the toilet.

I see that it is too small for me to fit through.

I see that the toilet cannot take me away, and I feel better.

I watch other people use the toilet.

I see that boys stand up when they go peepee.

They face the toilet, lift the seat, and peepee into the toilet bowl.

I see that girls sit down when they go peepee.

They sit on the toilet seat and peepee into the toilet bowl.

I see that both boys and girls sit down when they go poopoo.

They sit on the toilet seat and poopoo into the toilet bowl.

If I am not tall enough to use the toilet, I can go peepee and poopoo into a pottychair.

I ask someone to help me dump the peepee and poopoo into the toilet.

Sometimes I need help to go peepee and poopoo.

I need someone to help me take my pants down.

I need someone to help me pull them up.

After I use the toilet, I wipe my bottom with toilet paper.

I put the dirty toilet paper into the toilet bowl.

I flush the toilet.

I wash my hands.

I feel good that I did not go peepee and poopoo in my pants.